Presented to

_____

By

_____

On the occasion of

_____

LET THE
JOURNEY
BEGIN

FINDING GOD'S BEST FOR YOUR LIFE

MAX LUCADO

THOMAS NELSON
Since 1798

Let the Journey Begin

© 2009 by Max Lucado

Published in Nashville, Tennessee, by Thomas Nelson. Thomas Nelson is a registered trademark of HarperCollins Christian Publishing, Inc.

Thomas Nelson titles may be purchased in bulk for educational, business, fund-raising, or sales promotional use. For information, please e-mail SpecialMarkets@ThomasNelson.com.

Unless otherwise noted, all Scripture quotations are taken from the New Century Version®. Copyright © 2005 by Thomas Nelson. Used by permission. All rights reserved.

Scripture quotations marked NASB are taken from the New American Standard Bible® (NASB). Copyright © 1960, 1962, 1963, 1968, 1971, 1972, 1973, 1975, 1977, 1995 by The Lockman Foundation. Used by permission. www.Lockman.org.

Scripture quotations marked NEB are taken from the New English Bible. Copyright © Cambridge University Press and Oxford University Press 1961, 1970. All rights reserved.

Scripture quotations marked NIV are taken from the Holy Bible, New International Version®, NIV®. Copyright © 1973, 1978, 1984, 2011 by Biblica, Inc.® Used by permission of Zondervan. All rights reserved worldwide. www.zondervan.com. The "NIV" and "New International Version" are trademarks registered in the United States Patent and Trademark Office by Biblica, Inc.®

Scripture quotations markd NKJV are taken from New King James Version®. © 1982 by Thomas Nelson. Used by permission. All rights reserved.

Scripture quotations marked MSG are taken from THE MESSAGE. Copyright © 1993, 2002 by Eugene H. Peterson. Used by permission of NavPress. All rights reserved. Represented by Tyndale House Publishers, a Division of Tyndale House Ministries.

Scripture quotations marked PHILLIPS are from The New Testament in Modern English by J. B. Phillips. Copyright © 1960, 1972 J. B. Phillips. Administered by the Archbishops' Council of the Church of England. Used by permission.

Scripture quotations marked TLB are taken from The Living Bible. Copyright © 1971. Used by permission of Tyndale House Publishers, a Division of Tyndale House Ministries, Carol Stream, Illinois 60188. All rights reserved.

Scripture quotations marked TEV are taken from the Good News Translation in Today's English Version—Second Edition. Copyright © 1992 by American Bible Society. Used by permission.

Scripture quotations marked NLT are taken from the Holy Bible, New Living Translation. Copyright © 1996, 2004, 2007, 2015 by Tyndale House Foundation. Used by permission of Tyndale House Ministries, Carol Stream, Illinois 60188. All rights reserved.

Scripture quotations marked AMP are taken from the Amplified® Bible. ©1954, 1958, 1962, 1964, 1965, 1987 by The Lockman Foundation. Used by permission. www.Lockman.org.

ISBN 978-0-7180-3879-3 (eBook)
ISBN 978-0-7180-3049-0 (HC)
ISBN 978-1-4041-0686-4 (Custom)

Printed in United States of America

23 24 25 26 VER 18 17 16 15 14

TABLE OF CONTENTS

Stop, Look, and Listen—Good Habits for a Good Journey

A Fork in the Road—Deciding Which Way to Go

Dangers and Detours Ahead—Slow Down, Avoid Disaster

PREFACE

DEEP IN EVERY HEART YOU will find it: a longing for meaning, a quest for purpose.

If you ask the secularists, "What is the meaning of life?" they will say, "We don't know." At best they might agree that we are developed animals. At worst, rearranged space dust.

What a contrast to God's vision for life: "We are God's handiwork, created in Christ Jesus to devote ourselves to the good deeds for which God has designed us" (Ephesians 2:10 NEB).

God has placed his hand on your shoulder and said, "You're something special."

Untethered by time, he sees us all. In fact, he saw us before we were born.

And he loves what he sees. Flooded by emotion. Overcome by pride, the Starmaker turns to us, one by one, and says, "You are my child. I love you dearly."

And he loves us forever. Should you ever turn from him and walk away, he has already provided a way back. Nothing can separate you from his love. If you anchor these truths firmly in your heart, you will be ready for whatever you may encounter on the road ahead.

So let the journey begin!

Max Lucado

WHAT A GOD!

Ponder the achievement of God.
He doesn't condone our sin,
*   nor does he compromise his standard.*
He doesn't ignore our rebellion,
*   nor does he relax his demands.*
Rather than dismiss our sin, he assumes
*   our sin and, incredibly, sentences himself.*
God's holiness is honored.
*   Our sin is punished . . . and we are redeemed.*
God does what we cannot do so we can be
*   what we dare not dream: perfect before God.*

IN THE GRIP OF GRACE

God's Plan for the Journey of Life

A Road Map for Success

THE KEY QUESTION
IN LIFE IS NOT
"HOW STRONG AM I?"
BUT RATHER
"HOW STRONG
IS GOD?"

Direction for
the Road Ahead

OCCUPY YOURSELF WITH THE NATURE of God, not the size of your biceps . . .

That's what God told Moses to do. Remember the conversation at the burning bush? The tone was set in the first sentence. "Take off your sandals, because you are standing on holy ground" (Exodus 3:5). With these eleven words Moses is enrolled in a class on God. Immediately the roles are defined. God is holy. Approaching him on even a quarter-inch of leather is too pompous . . . No time is spent convincing Moses what Moses can do, but much time is spent explaining to Moses what God can do.

You and I tend to do the opposite. We would explain to Moses how he is ideally suited to return to Egypt . . . Then we'd remind Moses how perfect he is for wilderness travel . . . We'd spend time reviewing with Moses his résumé and strengths.

But God doesn't. The strength of Moses is never considered. No pep talk is given, no pats on the backs are offered. Not one word is spoken to recruit Moses. But many words are used to reveal God. The strength of Moses is not the issue; the strength of God is.

The Great House of God

3

NAILS
DIDN'T HOLD
GOD TO A
CROSS.
LOVE DID.

The Strength
of God's Love

"Can anything make me stop loving you?" God asks. "Watch me speak your language, sleep on your earth, and feel your hurts. Behold the maker of sight and sound as he sneezes, coughs, and blows his nose. You wonder if I understand how you feel? Look into the dancing eyes of the kid in Nazareth; that's God walking to school. Ponder the toddler at Mary's table; that's God spilling his milk.

"You wonder how long my love will last? Find your answer on a splintered cross, on a craggy hill. That's me you see up there, your maker, your God, nail-stabbed and bleeding. Covered in spit and sin-soaked. That's your sin I'm feeling. That's your death I'm dying. That's your resurrection I'm living. That's how much I love you."

In the Grip of Grace

YOU CHANGE YOUR
LIFE BY
CHANGING
YOUR HEART.

LOCKED
BEHIND BARS

THINK OF IT THIS WAY. Sin put you in prison. Sin locked you behind the bars of guilt and shame and deception and fear. Sin did nothing but shackle you to the wall of misery. Then Jesus came and paid your bail. He served your time; he satisfied the penalty and set you free. Christ died, and when you cast your lot with him, your old self died too.

The only way to be set free from the prison of sin is to serve its penalty. In this case the penalty is death. Someone has to die, either you or a heaven-sent substitute. You cannot leave prison unless there is a death. But that death has occurred at Calvary. And when Jesus died, you died to sin's claim on your life. You are free.

In the Grip of Grace

THOUGH WE WERE
SPIRITUALLY DEAD
BECAUSE OF THE THINGS
WE DID AGAINST GOD,
HE GAVE US NEW
LIFE WITH CHRIST.

EPHESIANS 2:5

A New Player
on Our Team

As youngsters, we neighborhood kids would play street football. The minute we got home from school, we'd drop the books and hit the pavement. The kid across the street had a dad with a great and a strong addiction to football. As soon as he'd pull in the driveway from work we'd start yelling for him to come and play ball. He couldn't resist. Out of fairness he'd always ask, "Which team is losing?" Then he would join that team, which often seemed to be mine.

His appearance in the huddle changed the whole ball game. He was confident, strong, and most of all, he had a plan. We'd circle around him, and he'd look at us and say, "Okay, boys, here is what we are going to do." The other side was groaning before we left the huddle. You see, we not only had a new plan, we had a new leader.

He brought new life to our team. God does precisely the same. We didn't need a new play; we needed a new plan. We didn't need to trade positions; we needed a new player. That player is Jesus Christ, God's firstborn son.

In the Grip of Grace

ANSWER THE BIG QUESTION
OF ETERNITY,
AND THE LITTLE QUESTIONS
OF LIFE FALL
INTO PERSPECTIVE.

Truth Will
Triumph

Imagine that you are an ice skater in competition. You are in first place with one more round to go. If you perform well, the trophy is yours. You are nervous, anxious, and frightened.

Then, only minutes before your performance, your trainer rushes to you with the thrilling news: "You've already won! The judges tabulated the scores, and the person in second place can't catch you. You are too far ahead."

Upon hearing that news, how will you feel? Exhilarated!

And how will you skate? Timidly? Cautiously? Of course not. How about courageously and confidently? You bet you will. You will do your best because the prize is yours. You will skate like a champion because that is what you are! You will hear the applause of victory . . .

The point is clear: the truth will triumph. The Father of truth will win, and the followers of truth will be saved.

The Applause of Heaven

FAITH IS THE GRIT
IN THE SOUL
THAT PUTS THE DARE
INTO DREAMS.

CHARACTER
CREATES COURAGE

A LEGEND FROM INDIA TELLS about a mouse who was terrified of cats until a magician agreed to transform him into a cat. That resolved his fear . . . until he met a dog, so the magician changed him into a dog. The mouse-turned-cat-turned-dog was content until he met a tiger—so, once again, the magician changed him into what he feared. But when the tiger came complaining that he had met a hunter, the magician refused to help. "I will make you into a mouse again, for though you have the body of a tiger, you still have the heart of a mouse."

Sound familiar? How many people do you know who have built a formidable exterior, only to tremble inside with fear? We tackle our anxieties by taking on the appearance of a tiger. We face our fears with force . . .

Or if we don't use force, we try other methods. We stockpile wealth. We seek security in things. We cultivate fame and seek status.

But do these approaches work? Can power, possessions, or popularity really deliver us from our fears?

Courage is an outgrowth of who we are. Exterior supports may temporarily sustain, but only inward character creates courage.

The Applause of Heaven

GOD WOULD PREFER WE HAVE AN OCCASIONAL LIMP THAN A PERPETUAL STRUT. AND IF IT TAKES A THORN FOR HIM TO MAKE HIS POINT, HE LOVES US ENOUGH NOT TO PLUCK IT OUT.

When God Says No

There are times when the one thing you want is the one thing you never get . . .

All you want is an open door or an extra day or an answered prayer, for which you will be thankful.

And so you pray and wait.

No answer.

You pray and wait.

No answer.

You pray and wait.

May I ask a very important question? What if God says no?

What if the request is delayed or even denied? When God says no to you, how will you respond? If God says, "I've given you my grace, and that is enough," will you be content?

Content. That's the word. A state of heart in which you would be at peace if God gave you nothing more than he already has. Test yourself with this question: What if God's only gift to you were his grace to save you? Would you be content?

What if his answer is, "My grace is enough." Would you be content?

You see, from heaven's perspective, grace is enough.

In the Grip of Grace

IF YOU WANT TO
TOUCH GOD'S HEART,
USE THE NAME HE LOVES
TO HEAR. CALL HIM FATHER.

WE ALL NEED A FATHER

[RECENTLY], MY DAUGHTER JENNA AND I spent several days in the old city of Jerusalem . . . One afternoon, as we were exiting the Jaffa gate, we found ourselves behind an orthodox Jewish family—a father and his three small girls. One of the daughters, perhaps four or five years of age, fell a few steps behind and couldn't see her father. Abba! she called to him. He stopped and looked. Only then did he realize he was separated from his daughter. Abba! she called again. He spotted her and immediately extended his hand . . .

He held her hand tightly in his as they descended the ramp . . . When the signal changed, he led her and her sisters through the intersection. In the middle of the street, he reached down and swung her up into his arms and continued their journey.

Isn't that what we all need? An *abba* who will hear when we call? Who will take our hand when we are weak? Who will guide us through the hectic intersections of life? Don't we all need an *abba* who will swing us up into his arms and carry us home? We all need a father.

The Great House of God

EVEN JESUS WAS GIVEN
A PORTION HE FOUND
HARD TO SWALLOW. BUT
WITH GOD'S HELP, HE DID.

Not Every Day Is a
Three-Cookie Day

Last night during family devotions, I called my daughters to the table and set a plate in front of each. In the center of the table I placed a collection of food: some fruit, some raw vegetables, and some Oreo cookies. "Every day," I explained, "God prepares for us a plate of experiences. What kind of plate do you most enjoy?"

The answer was easy. Sara put three cookies on her plate. Some days are like that, aren't they? Some days are "three-cookie days." Many are not. Sometimes our plate has nothing but vegetables—twenty-four hours of celery, carrots, and squash. Apparently God knows we need some strength, and though the portion may be hard to swallow, isn't it for our own good? Most days, however, have a bit of it all. Vegetables, which are healthy but dull. Fruit, which tastes better and we enjoy. And even an Oreo, which does little for our nutrition, but a lot for our attitude . . .

The next time your plate has more broccoli than apple pie, remember who prepared the meal. And the next time your plate has a portion you find hard to swallow, talk to God about it. Jesus did.

The Great House of God

DON'T ASK GOD
TO DO WHAT YOU WANT.
ASK GOD TO DO
WHAT IS RIGHT.

The Cure for
Disappointment

When God doesn't do what we want, it's not easy. Never has been. Never will be. But faith is the conviction that God knows more than we do about this life and he will get us through it. Remember, disappointment is cured by revamped expectations.

I like the story about the fellow who went to the pet store in search of a singing parakeet. Seems he was a bachelor and his house was too quiet. The store owner had just the bird for him, so the man bought it.

The next day the bachelor came home from work to a house full of music. He went to the cage to feed the bird and noticed for the first time that the parakeet had only one leg.

He felt cheated that he'd been sold a one-legged bird, so he called and complained.

"What do you want," the store owner responded, "a bird who can sing or a bird who can dance?"

Good question for times of disappointment.

In the Word with Max Lucado

GOD PROMISES GLADNESS

Nine times he promises it. And he promises it to an unlikely crowd:

- *"The poor in spirit."* Beggars in God's soup kitchen.
- *"Those who mourn."* Sinners Anonymous bound together by the truth of their introduction: "Hi, I am me. I'm a sinner."
- *"The meek."* Pawnshop pianos played by Van Cliburn. (He's so good no one notices the missing keys.)
- *"Those who hunger and thirst."* Famished orphans who know the difference between a TV dinner and a Thanksgiving feast.
- *"The merciful."* Winners of the million-dollar lottery who share the prize with their enemies.
- *"The pure in heart."* Physicians who love lepers and escape infection.
- *"The peacemakers."* Architects who build bridges with wood from a Roman cross.
- *"The persecuted."* Those who manage to keep an eye on heaven while walking through hell on earth.

It is to this band of pilgrims that God promises a special blessing. A heavenly joy. A sacred delight.

But this joy is not cheap. What Jesus promises is not a gimmick to give you goose bumps nor a mental attitude that has to be pumped up at pep rallies. No, Matthew 5 describes God's radical reconstruction of the heart.

The Applause of Heaven

GOD'S GLADNESS IS NOT RECEIVED BY THOSE WHO EARN IT, BUT BY THOSE WHO ADMIT THEY DON'T DESERVE IT.

Focus on the
Task at Hand

LIFE IS TOUGH ENOUGH AS IT IS. It's even tougher when we're headed in the wrong direction.

One of the incredible abilities of Jesus was to stay on target. His life never got off track. He had no money, no computers, no jets, no administrative assistants or staff; yet Jesus did what many of us fail to do. He kept his life on course.

As Jesus looked across the horizon of his future, he could see many targets. Many flags were flapping in the wind, each of which he could have pursued. He could have been a political revolutionary. He could have been a national leader. But in the end he chose to be a Savior and save souls.

Anyone near Christ for any length of time heard it from Jesus himself. "The Son of Man came to find lost people and save them" (Luke 19:10). "The Son of Man did not come to be served. He came to serve others and to give his life as a ransom for many people" (Mark 10:45).

The heart of Christ was relentlessly focused on one task. The day he left the carpentry shop of Nazareth he had one ultimate aim—the cross of Calvary. He was so focused that his final words were, "It is finished" (John 19:30).

How could Jesus say he was finished? There were still the

hungry to feed, the sick to heal, the untaught to instruct, and the unloved to love. How could he say he was finished? Simple. He had completed his designated task. His commission was fulfilled. The painter could set aside his brush, the sculptor lay down his chisel, the writer put away his pen. The job was done.

Wouldn't you love to be able to say the same? Wouldn't you love to look back on your life and know you had done what you were called to do?

Just Like Jesus

ENJOY SERVING THE LORD, AND HE WILL GIVE YOU WHAT YOU WANT. DEPEND ON THE LORD; TRUST HIM, AND HE WILL TAKE CARE OF YOU.

PSALM 37:4–5

Whose Dream Will
You Follow?

Let's be honest—there's a lot in life that doesn't make sense.

School. Friends. The news. Politics. Wall Street. Even God's track record in the Bible doesn't make a lot of sense:

- Transporting a million or so people across the desert for forty years to a mysterious promised land (Exodus–Deuteronomy)
- Whittling a thirty-two-thousand-man army down to three hundred in order to attack the most feared warriors in the land (Judges 7:1–16)
- Saving the world through a baby born in a barn (Luke 2:1–7) . . .

So if someone has a dream that makes perfect sense, it really couldn't be from God. That's not how he dreams!

We forget that *impossible* is one of God's favorite words. He dreams impossible dreams. Why?

If you accomplish a possible dream, then you get all the glory.

But if you accomplish an impossible dream, then God gets all the glory . . .

In the end you must ask yourself, whose dream am I going to follow: mine, my parents', or God's? God's dreams are always bigger and better and more unbelievable. His dreams look like these:

- Your neighbors . . . your community . . . your school coming to Christ
- Churches in your zip code coming together to pray for revival
- An end to hunger and disease in just one country
- Peace on earth

Dare to dream like God.

Max on Life

THE PURPOSE OF IMPOSSIBLE DREAMS IS TO SHOW THE WORLD THAT AN INCREDIBLE, UNBELIEVABLE GOD STILL EXISTS, AND HE WORKS IN THE LIVES OF PEOPLE.

NO MATTER WHO YOU ARE OR WHAT YOU'VE DONE, GOD CAN USE YOU.

Make a Difference
in Your World

If God chose only righteous people to change the world, you could count them all on one finger—Jesus. Instead, he included others in his plan—the sinners, the ungodly, the imperfect, the fearful, the prideful, the truth twisters. There's a lot more of us to choose from.

The reassuring lesson is clear. God used (and uses!) people to change the world. People! Not saints or superhumans or geniuses but people. Crooks, creeps, lovers, and liars—he uses them all. And what they lack in perfection, God makes up for in love.

If you ever wonder how God can use you to make a difference in your world, just look at those he has already used, and take heart.

Because you're imperfect, you can speak of making mistakes.

Because you're a sinner, you can speak of forgiveness.

God restores the broken and the brittle, then parades them before the world as trophies of his love and strength. The world sees the ungodly turn godly, and they know God must love them too.

Max on Life

Have You Lost Your Hearing?

Once there was a man who dared God to speak.
Burn the bush like you did for Moses, God.
And I will follow.
Collapse the walls like you did for Joshua, God.
And I will fight.
Still the waves like you did on Galilee, God.
And I will listen.
And so the man sat by a bush, near a wall, close to the
sea and waited for God to speak.
And God heard the man, so God answered.
He sent fire, not for a bush, but for a church.
He brought down a wall, not of brick, but of sin.
He stilled a storm, not of the sea, but of a soul.
And God waited for the man to respond.
And he waited . . .
And he waited . . .
And waited.
But because the man was looking at bushes, not hearts;
bricks and not lives, seas and not souls, he decided
that God had done nothing.
Finally he looked to God and asked,
Have you lost your power?
And God looked at him and said,
Have you lost your hearing?

A Gentle Thunder

STOP, LOOK, and LISTEN

———

Good Habits for a Good Journey

GROWTH IS THE GOAL
OF THE CHRISTIAN.
MATURITY IS
MANDATORY.

Healthy Habits

I LIKE THE STORY OF THE LITTLE BOY who fell out of bed. When his mom asked him what happened, he answered, "I don't know. I guess I stayed too close to where I got in."

Easy to do the same with our faith. It's tempting just to stay where we got in and never move.

Pick a time in the not-too-distant past. A year or two ago. Now ask yourself a few questions. How does your prayer life today compare with then? How about your giving? Have both the amount and the joy increased? What about your church loyalty? Can you tell you've grown? And Bible study? Are you learning to learn?

There they are. Healthy habits worth having. Isn't it good to know that some habits are good for you? Make them a part of your day and grow. Don't make the mistake of the little boy. Don't stay too close to where you got in. It's risky resting on the edge.

When God Whispers Your Name

YOUR PRAYER ON EARTH ACTIVATES GOD'S POWER IN HEAVEN, AND "GOD'S WILL IS DONE ON EARTH AS IT IS IN HEAVEN."

Prayers Are
Precious Jewels

You can talk to God because God listens. Your voice matters in heaven. He takes you very seriously. When you enter his presence, the attendants turn to you to hear your voice. No need to fear that you will be ignored. Even if you stammer or stumble, even if what you have to say impresses no one, it impresses God—and he listens . . .

Intently. Carefully. The prayers are honored as precious jewels. Purified and empowered, the words rise in a delightful fragrance to our Lord . . . Your words do not stop until they reach the very throne of God . . .

Your prayers move God to change the world. You may not understand the mystery of prayer. You don't need to. But this much is clear: Actions in heaven begin when someone prays on earth. What an amazing thought!

The Great House of God

Make a Plan

A DRAMATIC CRISIS REQUIRES A dramatic response, right? Not always.

We equate spirituality with high drama: Paul raising the dead, Peter healing the sick. Yet for every Paul and Peter, there are a dozen Josephs. Men and women blessed with skills of administration. Steady hands through whom God saves people. Joseph never raised the dead, but he kept people from dying. He never healed the sick, but he kept sickness from spreading. He made a plan and stuck with it. And because he did, the nation survived. He triumphed with a calm, methodical plan.

You can do the same. You can't control the weather. You aren't in charge of the economy. You can't undo the tsunami or unwreck the car, but you can map out a strategy. Remember, God is in this crisis. Ask him to give you an index card–sized plan, two or three steps you can take today.

Seek counsel from someone who has faced a similar challenge. Ask friends to pray. Look for resources. Reach out to a support group. Most importantly, make a plan . . .

You'd prefer a miracle for your crisis? You'd rather see the bread multiplied or the stormy sea turned glassy calm in a finger snap? God may do this.

Then again, he may tell you, "I'm with you. I can use this for good. Now let's make a plan." Trust him to help you.

You'll Get Through This

IN THE END IT'S NOT THE FLASHY AND FLAMBOYANT WHO SURVIVE. IT IS THOSE WITH STEADY HANDS AND SOBER MINDS.

SET YOUR COMPASS IN
THE RIGHT DIRECTION

IMAGINE YOUR REACTION IF I were to take a telephone book, open it up, and proclaim, *I have found a list of everyone who's on welfare!* Or what if I said, *Here is a list of college graduates!* Or, *This book will tell us who has a red car.* You'd probably say, "Now wait a minute—that's not the purpose of that book. You're holding a *telephone* book. Its purpose is simply to reveal the name and number of residents of a city during a certain time frame."

Only by understanding its purpose can I accurately use the telephone book. Only by understanding its purpose can I accurately use the Bible . . .

The purpose of the Bible is simply to proclaim God's plan to save his children. It asserts that man is lost and needs to be saved. And it communicates the message that Jesus is the God in the flesh sent to save his children.

Though the Bible was written over sixteen centuries by at least forty authors, it has one central theme—salvation through faith in Christ. Begun by Moses in the lonely desert of Arabia and finished by John on the lonely Isle of Patmos, it is held together by a strong thread: God's passion and God's plan to save his children.

What a vital truth! Understanding the purpose of the Bible is like setting the compass in the right direction. Calibrate it correctly and you'll journey safely. But fail to set it, and who knows where you'll end up.

In the Word with Max Lucado

THE PROBLEM IS
NOT THAT GOD HASN'T
SPOKEN BUT THAT
WE HAVEN'T LISTENED.

SOMEONE WHO SEES GRACE
AS PERMISSION TO SIN
HAS MISSED GRACE ENTIRELY.
MERCY UNDERSTOOD
IS HOLINESS DESIRED.

Grace Teaches Us
How to Live

Do we ever compromise tonight, knowing we'll confess tomorrow?

It's easy to be like the fellow visiting Las Vegas who called the preacher, wanting to know the hours of the Sunday service. The preacher was impressed. "Most people who come to Las Vegas don't do so to go to church."

"Oh, I'm not coming for the church. I'm coming for the gambling and parties and wild women. If I have half as much fun as I intend to, I'll need a church come Sunday morning."

Is that the intent of grace? Is God's goal to promote disobedience? Hardly. "Grace . . . teaches us not to live against God nor to do the evil things the world wants us to do. Instead, that grace teaches us to live in the present age in a wise and right way and in a way that shows we serve God" (Titus 2:11–12). God's grace has released us from selfishness. Why return?

In the Grip of Grace

Four Habits
Worth Having

How do you get rid of bad habits? By developing good ones. Here are four to start with:

First, the habit of prayer: "Base your happiness on your hope in Christ. When trials come endure them patiently, steadfastly maintain the *habit* of prayer" (Romans 12:12 PHILLIPS, emphasis mine). Posture, tone, and place are personal matters. Select the form that works for you. But don't think about it too much. Better to pray awkwardly than not at all.

Second, the habit of study: "The man who looks into the perfect mirror of God's law . . . and makes a *habit* of so doing, is not the man who sees and forgets. He puts that law into practice and he wins true happiness" (James 1:25 PHILLIPS, emphasis mine).

Third, the habit of giving: "On *every Lord's Day* each of you should put aside something from what you have earned during the week, and use it for this offering. The amount depends on how much the Lord has helped you earn" (1 Corinthians 16:2 TLB, emphasis mine). You don't give for God's sake. You give for your sake. "The purpose of tithing is to teach you always to put God first in your lives" (Deuteronomy 14:23 TLB).

And last of all, the habit of fellowship: "Let us not give up the *habit* of meeting together, as some are doing. Instead, let us encourage one another" (Hebrews 10:25 TEV, emphasis mine). You need support. You need what the Bible calls *fellowship*. And you need it every week.

Four habits worth having. Isn't it good to know that some habits are good for you?

Max on Life

GROW IN THE GRACE AND KNOWLEDGE OF OUR LORD AND SAVIOR JESUS CHRIST.

2 PETER 3:18 NIV

Exposed to a
Higher Standard

Most of my life I've been a closet slob. I was slow to see the logic of neatness. Why make up a bed if you are going to sleep in it again tonight? Does it make sense to wash dishes after only one meal? Isn't it easier to leave your clothes on the floor at the foot of the bed so they'll be there when you get up and put them on?

Then I got married . . .

I enrolled in a twelve-step program for slobs. ("My name is Max, and I hate to vacuum.") A physical therapist helped me rediscover the muscles used for hanging shirts and placing toilet paper on the holder. My nose was reintroduced to the fragrance of Pine Sol . . .

Then came the moment of truth. Denalyn went out of town for a week. Initially I reverted to the old man. I figured I'd be a slob for six days and clean on the seventh. But something strange happened, a curious discomfort. I couldn't relax with dirty dishes in the sink.

What had happened to me?

Simple. I'd been exposed to a higher standard.

Isn't that what has happened with us?

Before Christ our lives were out of control, sloppy, and indulgent. We didn't even know we were slobs until we met him . . .

Suddenly we find ourselves wanting to do good. Go back to the old mess? Are you kidding?

In the Grip of Grace

YOU WERE MADE FREE
FROM SIN, AND NOW YOU ARE
SLAVES TO GOODNESS.

ROMANS 6:17–18

THOSE WHO KEEP SECRETS
FROM GOD KEEP THEIR
DISTANCE FROM GOD.
THOSE WHO ARE HONEST
WITH GOD DRAW NEAR TO GOD.

THE BRIDGE OF
CONFESSION

ONCE THERE WERE A COUPLE OF FARMERS who couldn't get along with each other. A wide ravine separated their two farms, but as a sign of their mutual distaste for each other, each constructed a fence on his side of the chasm to keep the other out.

In time, however, the daughter of one met the son of the other, and the couple fell in love. Determined not to be kept apart by the folly of their fathers, they tore down the fence and used the wood to build a bridge across the ravine.

Confession does that. Confessed sin becomes the bridge over which we can walk back into the presence of God.

In the Grip of Grace

GOD LOVES MY NEIGHBOR AND MAKES HIM MY BROTHER.

ROCKING THE BOAT

GOD HAS ENLISTED US IN his navy and placed us on his ship. The boat has one purpose—to carry us safely to the other shore.

This is no cruise ship; it's a battleship. We aren't called to a life of leisure; we are called to a life of service. Each of us has a different task. Some, concerned with those who are drowning, are snatching people from the water. Others are occupied with the enemy, so they man the cannons of prayer and worship. Still others devote themselves to the crew, feeding and training the crew members.

Though different, we are the same. Each can tell of a personal encounter with the captain, for each has received a personal call. He found us among the shanties of the seaport and incited us to follow him. Our faith was born at the sight of his fondness, and so we went.

We each followed him across the gangplank of his grace onto the same boat. There is one captain and one destination. Though the battle is fierce, the boat is safe, for our captain is God. The ship will not sink. For that, there is no concern.

In the Grip of Grace

Honest to God

I made a mistake in high school . . .

Our baseball coach had a firm rule against chewing tobacco. We had a couple of players who were known to sneak a chew, and he wanted to call it to our attention.

He got our attention, all right. Before long we'd all tried it. A sure test of manhood was to take a chew when the pouch was passed down the bench. I had barely made the team; I sure wasn't going to fail the test of manhood.

One day I'd just popped a plug in my mouth when one of the players warned, "Here comes the coach!" Not wanting to get caught, I did what came naturally, I swallowed. *Gulp.*

I added new meaning to the scripture, "I felt weak deep inside me. I moaned all day long . . . My strength was gone as in the summer heat" (Psalm 32:3–4). I paid the price for hiding my disobedience.

My body was not made to ingest tobacco. Your soul was not made to ingest sin.

May I ask a frank question? Are you keeping any secrets from God? Any parts of your life off limits? Any cellars boarded up or attics locked? Any part of your past or present that you hope you and God never discuss?

Take a pointer from a nauseated third baseman. You'll feel better if you get it out.

In the Grip of Grace

IN THE GRIP OF GRACE,
YOU'RE FREE
TO BE HONEST.

WE DISCOVER GLADNESS
WHEN WE LEAVE THE PRISON
OF PRIDE AND REPENT
OF OUR REBELLION.

THE SOIL OF THE SOUL

CONFESSION DOES FOR THE SOUL what preparing the land does for the field. Before the farmer sows the seed, he works the acreage, removing the rocks and pulling the stumps. He knows that seed grows better if the land is prepared. Confession is the act of inviting God to walk the acreage of our hearts. "There is a rock of greed over here, Father; I can't budge it. And that tree of guilt near the fence? Its roots are long and deep. And may I show you some dry soil, too crusty for seed?" God's seed grows better if the soil of the heart is cleared.

And so the Father and the Son walk the field together; digging and pulling, preparing the heart for fruit. Confession invites the Father to work the soil of the soul.

Confession seeks pardon from God, not amnesty. Pardon presumes guilt; amnesty, derived from the same Greek word as *amnesia*, "forgets" the alleged offense without imputing guilt. Confession admits wrong and seeks forgiveness; amnesty denies wrong and claims innocence.

In the Grip of Grace

Do Good, Quietly

HYPOCRISY TURNS PEOPLE AGAINST GOD. So God has a no-tolerance policy.

Let's take hypocrisy as seriously as God does. How can we?

1. *Expect no credit for good deeds.* None. If no one notices, you aren't disappointed. If someone does, you give the credit to God. Ask yourself this question: If no one knew of the good I do, would I still do it? If not, you're doing it to be seen by people.
2. *Give financial gifts in secret.* Money stirs the phony within us. We like to be seen earning it. And we like to be seen giving it. So "when you give to someone in need, don't let your left hand know what your right hand is doing" (Matthew 6:3 NLT).
3. *Don't fake spirituality.* When you go to church, don't select a seat just to be seen or sing just to be heard. If you raise your hands in worship, raise holy ones, not showy ones. When you talk, don't doctor your vocabulary with trendy religious terms.

Bottom line: don't make a theater production out of your faith. "Watch me! Watch me!" is a call used on the playground, not in God's kingdom. Silence the trumpets. Cancel the parade. Enough with the name-dropping. If accolades come, politely deflect them before you believe them. Slay the desire to be noticed. Stir the desire to serve God.

Heed the counsel of Christ: "First wash the inside of the cup and the dish, and then the outside will become clean, too" (Matthew 23:26 NLT). Focus on the inside, and the outside will take care of itself. Lay your motives before God daily, hourly.

Do good things. Just don't do them to be noticed. You can be too good for your own good, you know.

Outlive Your Life

TO DO A GOOD THING IS A GOOD THING. TO DO GOOD TO BE SEEN IS NOT.

THE GRATEFUL HEART
IS LIKE A MAGNET
SWEEPING OVER THE DAY,
COLLECTING REASONS
FOR GRATITUDE.

Cultivate a
Grateful Heart

IF YOU FEEL THE WORLD OWES YOU something, brace yourself for a life of sour hours. You'll never get reimbursed. The sky will never be blue enough; the steak won't be cooked enough; the universe won't be good enough to deserve a human being like you. You'll snap and snarl your way to an early grave.

The grateful heart, on the other hand, sees each day as a gift.

Gratitude gets us through the hard stuff. To reflect on your blessings is to rehearse God's accomplishments. To rehearse God's accomplishments is to discover his heart. To discover his heart is to discover not just good gifts but the Good Giver. Gratitude always leaves us looking at God and away from dread. It does to anxiety what the morning sun does to valley mist. It burns it up.

You'll Get Through This

Keep a Regular
Date with God

A quiet time with God is very similar to a date. Here are some tools to help you keep your very special date with God.

Decide on *a regular time and place.* Select a slot in your schedule and a corner of your world, and claim it for God. A familiar place will remind you of similar feelings you experienced before with God. You need to get comfortable.

How much time should you take? As much as you need. Value quality over quantity. Your time with God should last long enough for you to say what you want and for God to say what he wants.

You should bring on your date *an open Bible*—God's Word, his love letter to you. You won't necessarily hear God speak out loud, but you can hear what he has to say through his eternal dialogue with humanity.

You also need *a listening heart.* Don't forget the admonition from James: "The man who looks into the perfect mirror of God's law, the law of liberty, and makes a habit of so doing, is not the man who sees and forgets. He puts that law into practice and he wins true happiness" (James 1:25 PHILLIPS). Listen to the lover of your soul. Don't just nod your head, pretending to hear. Your date knows when you're engaged. So does God.

Just as you wouldn't miss your date with a loved one, claiming you were too busy, make sure your date with God is on the calendar, and do everything in your power to keep it special.

Max on Life

MAKE GOD'S PRESENCE YOUR PASSION.

WORKS DONE IN
GOD'S NAME
LONG OUTLIVE
OUR EARTHLY LIVES.

Help Others,
Serve Jesus

*When we love those in need,
we are loving Jesus.*

IT IS A MYSTERY BEYOND SCIENCE, a truth beyond statistics. But it is a message that Jesus made crystal clear: when we love them, we love him.

I wonder if God creates people like Mother Teresa so he can prove his point: "See, you can do something today that will outlive your life."

There are several billion reasons to consider his challenge. Some of them live in your neighborhood; others live in jungles you can't find and have names you can't pronounce.

Some of them play in cardboard slums or sell sex on a busy street. Some of them walk three hours for water or wait all day for a shot of penicillin. Some of them brought their woes on themselves, and others inherited the mess from their parents.

None of us can help everyone. But all of us can help someone. And when we help them, we serve Jesus.

Who would want to miss a chance to do that?

Outlive Your Life

WHICH WILL BE
YOUR CHOICE?

On one side stands the crowd.
Jeering.
Baiting.
Demanding.
On the other stands a peasant.
Swollen lips.
Lumpy eye.
Lofty promise.
One promises acceptance, the other a cross.
One offers flesh and flash, the other offers faith.
The crowd challenges, "Follow us and fit in."
Jesus promises, "Follow me and stand out."
They promise to please.
God promises to save . . .
God looks at you and asks . . .
Which will be your choice?

A Gentle Thunder

A Fork in the Road

Deciding Which Way to Go

CLAIMING THEMSELVES
TO BE WISE WITHOUT GOD,
THEY BECAME UTTER
FOOLS INSTEAD.

ROMANS 1:22 TLB

THE PURPOSE OF LIFE

MINE DEEP ENOUGH IN EVERY HEART and you'll find it: a longing for meaning, a quest for purpose. As surely as a child breathes, he will someday wonder, *What is the purpose of my life?*

Some search for meaning in a career. "My purpose is to be a dentist." Fine vocation, but hardly a justification for existence. They opt to be a human "doing" rather than a human "being." Who they are is what they do; consequently they do a lot. They work many hours because if they don't work, they don't have an identity.

For others, who they are is what they have. They find meaning in a new car or a new house or new clothes. These people are great for the economy and rough on the budget because they are always seeking meaning in something they own . . .

Some try sports, entertainment, cults, sex, you name it.

All mirages in the desert of purpose . . .

Shouldn't we face the truth? If we don't acknowledge God, we are flotsam in the universe.

In the Grip of Grace

GOD IS NOT THE GOD OF CONFUSION, AND WHEREVER HE SEES SINCERE SEEKERS WITH CONFUSED HEARTS, YOU CAN BET YOUR SWEET DECEMBER THAT HE WILL DO WHATEVER IT TAKES TO HELP THEM SEE HIS WILL.

Knowing God's Will

We learn God's will by spending time in his presence. The key to knowing God's heart is having a relationship with him. A *personal* relationship. God will speak to you differently than he will speak to others. Just because God spoke to Moses through a burning bush, that doesn't mean we should all sit next to a bush waiting for God to speak. God used a fish to convict Jonah. Does that mean we should have worship services at Sea World? No. God reveals his heart personally to each person.

For that reason, your walk with God is essential. His heart is not seen in an occasional chat or weekly visit. We learn his will as we take up residence in his house every single day . . . Walk with him long enough and you come to know his heart.

The Great House of God

ACTIONS
HAVE CONSEQUENCES.

Do What Pleases God

Do what pleases God. Your coworkers want to include a trip to a gentleman's club on the evening agenda. What do you do? *Do what pleases God.* Your date invites you to conclude the evening with drinks at his apartment. How should you reply? *Do what pleases God.* Your friends hand you a joint of marijuana to smoke; your classmates show you a way to cheat; the Internet provides pornography to watch—ask yourself the question: How can I please God? "Do what is right as a sacrifice to the Lord and trust the Lord" (Psalm 4:5).

You don't fix a struggling marriage with an affair, a drug problem with more drugs, debt with more debt. You don't fix stupid with stupid. You don't get out of a mess by making another one. *Do what pleases God.* You will never go wrong doing what is right . . .

Turbulent times will tempt you to forget God. Shortcuts will lure you. Sirens will call you. But don't be foolish or naive. Do what pleases God. Nothing more, nothing less.

You'll Get Through This

Prepare for the
Unknown

Like a pilot before takeoff, I always go over my preflight checklist before I take any trips into the unknown. I ask myself:

Where has God taken me before? I look at my passport, remembering all the exciting and adventurous places God has sent me in the past. I remember the experiences I faced, the cultures I embraced, the lifestyles I encountered. Then I consider how often God uprooted folks in Scripture. Who better to confront Pharaoh than an Egyptian-raised Jew? Who better to lead Israel than a shepherd-trained warrior? Who better to bridge the gap between deep thinkers and deep believers than a Roman-trained ex-Pharisee? God uses past experiences to overcome present problems.

Ask yourself, where has God taken me before?

What trips am I passionate about? Some people get excited about going to Hawaii. Others, Toledo. Many think Alaska is too cold. Others feel the Bahamas are too hot. We all have different passions and burdens. Some like to preach in foreign countries. Others like to help their neighbors. Some hurt for gang members and drug dealers. Others weep over Wall Street and Capitol Hill.

Ask yourself, what people and places am I most passionate about?

Am I a pilot, a flight attendant, a mechanic, or a baggage handler? I never see the pilot percolating coffee or the attendant with a screwdriver under the airplane's hood. Why? Because we all have something we are good at, and we are expected to do that one thing well. Pilots take people places. Flight attendants serve. Mechanics make sure everything is working well behind the scenes. Baggage handlers carry other people's burdens.

Think about it: What is your purpose?

Once you've checked off the . . .

- previous places,
- present passions,
- professional purpose,

you are ready to fly!

Max on Life

THE LORD HAS ASSIGNED TO EACH HIS TASK.

1 Corinthians 3:5 NIV

I Choose Love

It's quiet. It's early. My coffee is hot. The sky is still black. The world is still asleep. The day is coming.

In a few moments the day will arrive. It will roar down the track with the rising of the sun. The stillness of the dawn will be exchanged for the noise of the day. The calm of solitude will be replaced by the pounding pace of the human race. The refuge of the early morning will be invaded by decisions to be made and deadlines to be met.

For the next twelve hours I will be exposed to the day's demands. It is now that I must make a choice. Because of Calvary, I'm free to choose. And so I choose.

I choose love. No occasion justifies hatred; no injustice warrants bitterness. I choose love. Today I will love God and what God loves.

I choose joy. I will invite my God to be the God of circumstance. I will refuse the temptation to be cynical . . . the tool of the lazy thinker. I will refuse to see people as anything less than human beings, created by God. I will refuse to see any problem as anything less than an opportunity to see God.

I choose peace. I will live forgiven. I will forgive so that I may live.

I choose patience. I will overlook the inconveniences of the world. Instead of cursing the one who takes my place, I'll invite him to do so. Rather than complain that the wait is too long, I will thank God for a moment to pray. Instead of clinching my fist at new assignments, I will face them with joy and courage.

I choose kindness. I will be kind to the poor, for they are alone. Kind to the rich, for they are afraid. And kind to the unkind, for such is how God has treated me.

I choose goodness. I will go without a dollar before I take a dishonest one. I will be overlooked before I will boast. I will confess before I will accuse. I choose goodness.

I choose faithfulness. Today I will keep my promises. My debtors will not regret their trust. My associates will not question my word. My wife will not question my love. And my children will never fear that their father will not come home.

I choose gentleness. Nothing is won by force. I choose to be gentle. If I raise my voice, may it be only in praise. If I clench my fist, may it be only in prayer. If I make a demand, may it be only of myself.

I choose self-control. I am a spiritual being. After this body is dead, my spirit will soar. I refuse to let what will rot, rule the eternal. I choose self-control. I will be drunk only by joy. I will be impassioned only by my faith. I will be influenced only by God. I will be taught only by Christ. I choose self-control.

Love, joy, peace, patience, kindness, goodness, faithfulness, gentleness, and self-control. To these I commit my day. If I succeed, I will give thanks. If I fail, I will seek his grace. And then, when this day is done, I will place my head on my pillow and rest.

When God Whispers Your Name

THE FIRE OF YOUR HEART
IS THE LIGHT
OF YOUR PATH.

The Fire of
Your Heart

WANT TO KNOW GOD'S WILL for your life? Then answer this question: What ignites your heart? Forgotten orphans? Untouched nations? The inner city? The outer limits?

Heed the fire within!

Do you have a passion to sing? Then sing!

Are you stirred to manage? Then manage!

Do you ache for the ill? Then treat them!

Do you hurt for the lost? Then teach them!

As a young man I felt the call to preach. Unsure if I was correct in my reading of God's will for me, I sought the counsel of a minister I admired. His counsel still rings true. "Don't preach," he said, "unless you have to."

As I pondered his words I found my answer: "I have to. If I don't, the fire will consume me."

What is the fire that consumes you?

The Great House of God

SUCCEED
IN WHAT MATTERS.

A Passion for
Excellence

THE PUSH FOR POWER HAS come to shove. And most of us are either pushing or being pushed.

I might point out the difference between a passion for excellence and a passion for power. The desire for excellence is a gift of God, much needed in society. It is characterized by respect for quality and a yearning to use God's gifts in a way that pleases him.

There are certain things you can do that no one else can. Perhaps it is parenting, or constructing houses, or encouraging the discouraged. There are things that *only you* can do, and you are alive to do them. In the great orchestra we call life, you have an instrument and a song, and you owe it to God to play them both sublimely.

But there is a canyon of difference between doing your best to glorify God and doing whatever it takes to glorify yourself. The quest for excellence is a mark of maturity. The quest for power is childish.

The Applause of Heaven

You Are One
of a Kind

In my closet hangs a sweater that I seldom wear. It is too small. The sleeves are too short, the shoulders too tight. Some of the buttons are missing, and the thread is frazzled. Logic says I should clear out the space and get rid of the sweater.

That's what logic says.

But love won't let me.

Something unique about that sweater makes me keep it. What is unusual about it? It's the creation of a devoted mother expressing her love.

That sweater is unique. One of a kind. It can't be replaced. Each strand was chosen with care. Each thread was selected with affection.

And though the sweater has lost all of its use, it has lost none of its value. It is valuable not because of its function, but because of its maker.

That must have been what the psalmist had in mind when he wrote, "You knit me together in my mother's womb" (Psalm 139:13 NIV).

Think on those words. You were knitted together. You aren't an accident. You weren't mass-produced. You aren't an assembly-line product. You were deliberately planned, specifically gifted, and lovingly positioned on this earth by the Master Craftsman.

In a society that has little room for second fiddles, that's good news . . . In a system that ranks the value of a human by the figures of his salary or the shape of her legs . . . let me tell you something: Jesus' plan is a reason for joy!

The Applause of Heaven

NO ONE IS
USELESS TO GOD.
NO ONE.

WE ARE GOD'S HANDIWORK,
CREATED IN CHRIST JESUS
TO DEVOTE OURSELVES
TO THE GOOD DEEDS FOR
WHICH GOD HAS DESIGNED US.

EPHESIANS 2:10 NEB

GOD'S SIGNATURE
MAKES YOU SPECIAL

WITH GOD IN YOUR WORLD, you aren't an accident or an incident; you are a gift to the world, a divine work of art, signed by God.

One of the finest gifts I ever received is a football signed by thirty former professional quarterbacks. There is nothing unique about this ball. For all I know it was bought at a discount sports store. What makes it unique are the signatures.

The same is true with us. In the scheme of nature *Homo sapiens* are not unique. We aren't the only creatures with flesh and hair and blood and hearts. What makes us special is not only our body but the signature of God on our lives. We are his works of art. We are created in his image to do good deeds. We are significant, not because of what we do, but because of whose we are.

In the Grip of Grace

JUST BECAUSE YOU
UNDERSTAND THE SYSTEM,
THAT DOESN'T DENY THE
PRESENCE OF SOMEONE
OUTSIDE THE SYSTEM.

Got It All
Figured Out

WE UNDERSTAND HOW STORMS ARE CREATED. We map solar systems and transplant hearts. We measure the depths of the oceans and send signals to distant planets. We have studied the system and are learning how it works.

And, for some, the loss of mystery has led to the loss of majesty. The more we know, the less we believe. Strange, don't you think? Knowledge of the workings shouldn't negate wonder. Knowledge should stir wonder. Who has more reason to worship than the astronomer who has seen the stars? Than the surgeon who has held a heart? Than the oceanographer who has pondered the depths? The more we know, the more we should be amazed.

Ironically, the more we know, the less we worship. We are more impressed with our discovery of the light switch than with the one who invented electricity . . . Rather than worship the Creator, we worship the creation (Romans 1:25).

No wonder there is no wonder. We've figured it all out.

In the Grip of Grace

Restored Hope
Along the Way

WHAT WOULD IT TAKE TO restore your hope? What would you need to reenergize your journey?

Though the answers are abundant, three come quickly to mind.

The first would be a person. Not just any person. You don't need someone equally confused. You need someone who knows the way out.

And from him you need some vision. You need someone to lift your spirits. You need someone to look you in the face and say, "This isn't the end. Don't give up. There is a better place than this. And I'll lead you there." And, perhaps most important, you need direction. If you have only a person but no renewed vision, all you have is company. If he has a vision but no direction, you have a dreamer for company. But if you have a person with direction—who can take you from this place to the right place—ah, then you have one who can restore your hope.

Or, to use David's words, "He restores my soul" (Psalm 23:3 NASB). Our Shepherd majors in restoring hope to the soul. Whether you are a lamb lost on a craggy ledge or a city slicker alone in a deep jungle, everything changes when your rescuer appears.

Your loneliness diminishes, because you have fellowship.

Your despair decreases, because you have vision. Your confusion begins to lift, because you have direction.

Please note: you haven't left the jungle. The trees still eclipse the sky, and the thorns still cut the skin. Animals lurk and rodents scurry. The jungle is still a jungle. It hasn't changed, but you have. You have changed because you have hope. And you have hope because you have met someone who can lead you out.

Your Shepherd knows that you were not made for this place. He knows you are not equipped for this place. So he has come to guide you out.

Traveling Light

WHO ARE THOSE WHO
FEAR THE LORD?
HE WILL SHOW THEM THE PATH
THEY SHOULD CHOOSE.

PSALM 25:12 NLT

THE CONCLUSION IS
UNAVOIDABLE: SELF-SALVATION
SIMPLY DOES NOT WORK.

God's Highest Dream

Please note: Salvation is God-given, God-driven, God-empowered, and God-originated. The gift is not from man to God. It is from God to man. "It is not our love for God; it is God's love for us in sending his Son to be the way to take away our sins" (1 John 4:10).

We have attempted to reach the moon but scarcely made it off the ground. We tried to swim the Atlantic, but couldn't get beyond the reef. We have attempted to scale the Everest of salvation, but we have yet to leave the base camp, much less ascend the slope. The quest is simply too great; we don't need more supplies or muscle or technique; we need a helicopter.

Can't you hear it hovering?

"God has a way to *make people right with him*" (Romans 3:21, emphasis mine). How vital that we embrace this truth. God's highest dream is not to make us rich, not to make us successful or popular or famous. God's dream is to make us right with him.

In the Grip of Grace

SMOOTH SAILING
THROUGH LIFE'S STORMS

A FEW DAYS BEFORE OUR WEDDING, Denalyn and I enjoyed and endured a sailing voyage. Milt, a Miami church friend, had invited Denalyn, her mom, and me to join him and a few others on a leisurely cruise along the Florida coast.

Initially it was just that. Leisure. We stretched out on cushions, hung feet over the side, caught some ZZZs and rays. Nice. But then came the storm. The sky darkened, the rain started, and the flat ocean humped like a dragon's neck. Sudden waves of water tilted the vessel up until we saw nothing but sky and then downward until we saw nothing but blue. I learned this about sailing: there is nothing swell about a swell. Tanning stopped. Napping ceased. Eyes turned first to the thunderclouds, then to the captain. We looked to Milt.

He was deliberate and decisive. He told some people where to sit, others what to do, and all of us to hang on. And we did what he said. Why? We knew he knew best. No one else knew the difference between starboard and stern. Only Milt did. We trusted him. We knew he knew.

And we knew we didn't. Prior to the winds, we might have boasted about Boy Scout merit badges in sailing or bass-boat excursions. But once the storm hit, we shut up. (Except for Denalyn, who threw up.) We had no choice but to trust Milt. He knew what we didn't—and he cared. The vessel was captained, not by a hireling or a stranger, but by a pal. Our safety mattered to him. So we trusted him.

Oh that the choice were equally easy in life. Need I remind you about your westerly winds? With the speed of lightning and the force of a thunderclap, williwaws anger tranquil waters. Victims of sudden storms populate unemployment lines and ICU wards. You know the winds. You've felt the waves. Good-bye, smooth sailing. Hello, rough waters.

Such typhoons test our trust in the Captain. Does God know what he is doing? Can he get us out? Why did he allow the storm? The conditions worsen, and his instructions perplex: he calls on you to endure disaster, tolerate criticism, forgive an enemy . . . How do you respond?

Can you say about God what I said about Milt?

I know God knows what's best.

I know I don't.

I know he cares.

Such words come easily when the water is calm. But when you're looking at a wrecked car or a suspicious-looking mole, when war breaks out or thieves break in, do you trust him? If yes, then you're scoring high marks in the classroom of sovereignty.

This important biblical phrase defines itself. Zero in on the middle portion of the term. See the word within the word? *Sove-reign-ty.* To confess the sovereignty of God is to acknowledge the reign of God, his regal authority and veto power over everything that happens. To embrace God's sovereignty is to drink from the well of his lordship and make a sailboat-in-the-storm decision.

Come Thirsty

When You Need
Wisdom

How can I find godly wisdom to make good choices?

Surely you would listen to cooking suggestions from a five-star chef and remodeling tips from an expert handyman even though they weren't Christians. Wisdom is wisdom, and it comes in all shapes and sizes from all kinds of people.

But when the words of the world fall short, *go to the Lord.*

> *I will guide you along the best pathway for your life.*
> *I will advise you and watch over you.* (Psalm 32:8 NLT)

> *Seek his will in all you do,*
> *and he will show you which path to take.*
> (Proverbs 3:6 NLT)

> *My sheep listen to my voice; I know them, and they follow me.* (John 10:27 NLT)

Then *go to the Bible.*

> *For the word of God is living and active. Sharper than any double-edged sword, it penetrates even*

to dividing soul and spirit, joints and marrow;
it judges the thoughts and attitudes of the heart.
(Hebrews 4:12 NIV)

God's Word is a living and active counselor in your time of need.

So listen to your parents; then go to the Lord and his living Word. You can't go wrong with that combination.

Max on Life

THE FIFTH COMMANDMENT DOES NOT SAY, "HONOR YOUR GOD-FEARING MOTHER AND FATHER WHO HAVE A CHRISTIAN WORLDVIEW." IT SAYS, "HONOR YOUR FATHER AND YOUR MOTHER."

FOLLOW GOD'S LEADING

SOME YEARS AGO DENALYN AND I were a signature away from moving from one house to another. The structure was nice, and the price was fair. It seemed a wise move. But I didn't feel peaceful about it. The project stirred unease and restlessness. I finally drove to the builder's office and removed my name from his list. To this day I can't pinpoint the source of the discomfort. I just didn't feel peaceful about it.

Later I was asked to speak at a racial unity conference. I intended to decline but couldn't bring myself to do so. The event kept surfacing in my mind like a cork in a lake. Finally I agreed. Returning from the event, I still couldn't explain the impression to be there. But I felt peaceful about the decision, and that was enough.

Sometimes a choice just "feels" right. When Luke justified the writing of his gospel to Theophilus, he said, "Since I myself have carefully investigated everything from the beginning, it seemed good also to me to write an orderly account for you, most excellent Theophilus" (Luke 1:3 NIV).

Did you note the phrase "it seemed good also to me"? These words reflect a person standing at the crossroads. Luke pondered his options and selected the path that "seemed good."

Jude did likewise. He intended to dedicate his epistle to

the topic of salvation, but he felt uneasy with the choice. Look at the third verse of his letter:

> Dear friends, I wanted very much to write you about the salvation we all share. But I felt the need to write you about something else: I want to encourage you to fight hard for the faith that was given the holy people of God once and for all time.

Again the language. "I wanted . . . But I felt . . ." From whence came Jude's feelings? Did they not come from God? The same God who "is working in you to help you want to do . . . what pleases him" (Philippians 2:13). God creates the "want to" within us.

Be careful with this. People have been known to justify stupidity based on a feeling. "I felt God leading me to cheat on my wife . . . disregard my bills . . . lie to my boss . . . flirt with my married neighbor." Mark it down: God will not lead you to violate his Word. He will not contradict his teaching. Be careful with the phrase "God led me . . ." Don't banter it about. Don't disguise your sin as a leading of God. He will not lead you to lie, cheat, or hurt.

But he will faithfully lead you through the words of his Scripture and the advice of his faithful.

Max on Life

GODLESSNESS

The word defines itself. A life minus God. Worse than a disdain for God, this is a disregard for God.

A disdain at least acknowledges his presence. Godlessness doesn't.

Whereas disdain will lead people to act with irreverance, disregard causes them to act as if God were irrelevant, as if he were not a factor in the journey.

In the Grip of Grace

Dangers and Detours Ahead

Slow Down, Avoid Disaster

THE RIGHT HEART WITH
THE WRONG CREED
IS BETTER THAN THE
RIGHT CREED WITH
THE WRONG HEART.

GODLESS LIVING

SINCE THE HEDONIST HAS NEVER seen the hand who made the universe, he assumes there is no life beyond the here and now. He believes there is no truth beyond this room. No purpose beyond his own pleasure. No divine factor. He has no concern for the eternal . . .

What happens when a culture settles for grass huts instead of the father's castle? Are there any consequences for a godless pursuit of pleasure? Is there a price to pay for living for today?

The hedonist says, "Who cares? I may be bad, but so what? What I do is my business." He's more concerned about satisfying his passions than in knowing the Father. His life is so desperate for pleasure that he has no time or room for God.

Is he right? Is it OK to spend our days thumbing our noses at God and living it up?

Paul says, "Absolutely not!"

According to Romans 1, we lose more than stained-glass windows when we dismiss God. We lose our standard, our purpose, and our worship. "Their thinking became useless. Their foolish minds were filled with darkness. They said they were wise, but they became fools" (Romans 1:21–22).

In the Grip of Grace

YOU WILL NEVER
FORGIVE ANYONE
MORE THAN GOD HAS
ALREADY FORGIVEN YOU.

Revenge Is a
Raging Fire

RESENTMENT IS THE COCAINE OF the emotions. It causes our blood to pump and our energy level to rise.

But, also like cocaine, it demands increasingly larger and more frequent dosages. There is a dangerous point at which anger ceases to be an emotion and becomes a driving force. A person bent on revenge moves unknowingly further and further away from being able to forgive, for to be without the anger is to be without a source of energy.

That explains why the bitter complain to anyone who will listen. They want—they need—to have their fire fanned . . . Resentment is like cocaine in another way too. Cocaine can kill the addict. And anger can kill the angry . . .

And it can be spiritually fatal too. It shrivels the soul.

Hatred is the rabid dog that turns on its owner. Revenge is the raging fire that consumes the arsonist. Bitterness is the trap that snares the hunter.

And mercy is the choice that can set them all free.

The Applause of Heaven

GOD FORGETS THE PAST.
IMITATE HIM.

Do You Have a Hole
in Your Heart?

PERHAPS THE WOUND IS OLD. A parent abused you. A teacher slighted you . . .

And you are angry.

Or perhaps the wound is fresh. The friend who owes you money just drove by in a new car. The boss who hired you with promises of promotions has forgotten how to pronounce your name. Your circle of friends escaped on a weekend getaway, and you weren't invited . . .

And you are hurt.

Part of you is broken, and the other part is bitter. Part of you wants to cry, and part of you wants to fight. The tears you cry are hot because they come from your heart, where there is a fire burning. It's the fire of anger. It's blazing. It's consuming. Its flames leap up under a steaming pot of revenge.

And you are left with a decision. "Do I put the fire out or heat it up? Do I get over it or get even? Do I release it or resent it? Do I let my hurts heal, or do I let hurt turn into hate?" . . . Resentment is the deliberate decision to nurse the offense until it becomes a black, furry, growling grudge . . .

Unfaithfulness is wrong. Revenge is bad. But the worst part of all is that, without forgiveness, bitterness is all that is left.

The Applause of Heaven

CONFLICT IS
INEVITABLE, BUT
COMBAT IS OPTIONAL.

THE ANSWER TO
ARGUMENTS

SOMETIME AGO MY WIFE BOUGHT a monkey. I didn't want a monkey in our house, so I objected.

"Where is he going to eat?" I asked.

"At our table."

"Where is he going to sleep?" I inquired.

"In our bed."

"What about the odor?" I demanded.

"I got used to you; I guess the monkey can too."

Unity doesn't begin in examining others but in examining self. Unity begins not in demanding that others change, but in admitting that we aren't so perfect ourselves . . .

The answer to arguments? Acceptance. The first step to unity? Acceptance. Not agreement, acceptance. Not unanimity, acceptance. Not negotiation, arbitration, or elaboration. Those might come later but only after the first step, acceptance.

In the Grip of Grace

THE MORE WE IMMERSE OURSELVES IN GRACE, THE MORE LIKELY WE ARE TO GIVE GRACE.

Hatred Will
Break Your Back

Oh, the gradual grasp of hatred. Its damage begins like the crack in my windshield. Thanks to a speeding truck on a gravel road, my window was chipped. With time the nick became a crack, and the crack became a winding tributary. Soon the windshield was a spider web of fragments. I couldn't drive my car without thinking of the jerk who drove too fast. Though I've never seen him, I could describe him. He is some deadbeat bum who cheats on his wife, drives with a six-pack on the seat, and keeps the television so loud the neighbors can't sleep. His carelessness blocked my vision. (Didn't do much for my view out the windshield either.)

Ever heard the expression "blind rage"?

Let me be very clear. Hatred will sour your outlook and break your back. The load of bitterness is simply too heavy. Your knees will buckle under the strain, and your heart will break beneath the weight. The mountain before you is steep enough without the heaviness of hatred on your back. The wisest choice—the only choice—is for you to drop the anger. You will never be called upon to give anyone more grace than God has already given you.

In the Grip of Grace

Looking Forward in Faith

Some of us have postgraduate degrees from the University of Anxiety. We go to sleep worried that we won't wake up; we wake up worried that we didn't sleep. We worry that someone will discover that lettuce was fattening all along. The mother of one teenager bemoaned, "My daughter doesn't tell me anything. I'm a nervous wreck." Another mother replied, "My daughter tells me everything. I'm a nervous wreck." Wouldn't you love to stop worrying? Could you use a strong shelter from life's harsh elements?

God offers you just that: the possibility of a worry-free life. Not just less worry, but no worry. He created a dome for your heart. "His peace will guard your hearts and minds as you live in Christ Jesus" (Philippians 4:7 NLT).

Interested? Then take a good look at the rest of the passage.

Don't worry about anything; instead, pray about everything. Tell God what you need, and thank him for all he has done. Then you will experience God's peace, which exceeds anything we can understand. His peace will guard your hearts and minds as you live in Christ Jesus. (vv. 6–7)

The Christians in Philippi needed a biosphere. Attacks were coming at them from all angles. Preachers served for selfish gain (1:15–17). Squabbling church members threatened the unity of the church (4:2). False teachers preached a crossless gospel (3:2–3, 18–19). Some believers struggled to find food and shelter (4:19). Persecutions outside. Problems inside.

Enough hornets nests to make you worry. Folks in Philippi had them. Folks today have them. To them and us God gives the staggering proposal: "Don't worry about anything."

Yeah, right. And while I'm at it, I'll leapfrog the moon. Are you kidding?

Jesus isn't. Two words summarize his opinion of worry: irrelevant and irreverent.

Can all your worries add a single moment to your life? Of course not. Worry is irrelevant. It alters nothing. When was the last time you solved a problem by worrying about it? Imagine someone saying, "I got behind in my bills, so I resolved to worry my way out of debt. And, you know, it worked! A few sleepless nights, a day of puking and hand wringing. I yelled at my kids and took some pills, and—glory to worry—money appeared on my desk."

It doesn't happen! Worry changes nothing. You don't add one day to your life or one bit of life to your day by worrying.

But how can we stop doing so? Paul offers a two-pronged answer: God's part and our part. Our part includes prayer and gratitude. "Don't worry about anything; instead, pray about everything. Tell God what you need, and *thank him* for all he has done" (Philippians 4:6, emphasis mine).

Want to worry less? Then pray more. Rather than look forward in fear, look upward in faith.

Come Thirsty

SETTLING THE SCORE
IS DONE AT
GREAT EXPENSE.

The High Cost of
Getting Even

Have you ever noticed in the western movies how the bounty hunter travels alone? It's not hard to see why. Who wants to hang out with a guy who settles scores for a living? Who wants to risk getting on his bad side? More than once I've heard a person spew his anger. He thought I was listening, when really I was thinking, *I hope I never get on his list.* Cantankerous sorts, these bounty hunters. Best leave them alone. Hang out with the angry and you might catch a stray bullet. Debt-settling is a lonely occupation. It's also an unhealthy one.

If you're out to settle the score, you'll never rest. How can you? For one thing, your enemy may never pay up. As much as you think you deserve an apology, your debtor may not agree. The racist may never repent. The chauvinist may never change. As justified as you are in your quest for vengeance, you may never get a penny's worth of justice. And if you do, will it be enough?

The Great House of God

A STAMMERING SHEPHERD
IN THIS GENERATION
MAY BE THE MIGHTY
MOSES OF THE NEXT.

GET OUT OF THE
JUDGMENT SEAT

WE CONDEMN A MAN FOR stumbling this morning, but we didn't see the blows he took yesterday. We judge a woman for the limp in her walk, but cannot see the tack in her shoe. We mock the fear in their eyes, but have no idea how many stones they have ducked or darts they have dodged.

Are they too loud? Perhaps they fear being neglected again. Are they too timid? Perhaps they fear failing again. Too slow? Perhaps they fell the last time they hurried. You don't know. Only one who has followed yesterday's steps can be their judge.

Not only are we ignorant about yesterday, we are ignorant about tomorrow. Dare we judge a book while chapters are yet unwritten? Should we pass a verdict on a painting while the artist still holds the brush? How can you dismiss a soul until God's work is complete? "God began doing a good work in you, and I am sure he will continue it until it is finished when Jesus Christ comes again" (Philippians 1:6).

In the Grip of Grace

GOD'S DELIGHT IS
RECEIVED UPON
SURRENDER, NOT
AWARDED UPON CONQUEST.

Mountains You Weren't
Made to Climb

THERE ARE CERTAIN MOUNTAINS only God can climb.

It's not that you aren't welcome to try, it's just that you aren't able.

If the word *Savior* is in your job description, it's because you put it there. Your role is to help the world, not save it. Mount Messiah is one mountain you weren't made to climb.

Nor is Mount Self-Sufficient. You aren't able to run the world, nor are you able to sustain it. Some of you think you can. You are self-made. You don't bow your knees, you just roll up your sleeves and put in another twelve-hour day . . . which may be enough when it comes to making a living or building a business. But when you face your own grave or your own guilt, your power will not do the trick.

You were not made to run a kingdom, nor are you expected to be all-powerful. And you certainly can't handle all the glory. Mount Applause is the most seductive of the three peaks. The higher you climb, the more people applaud, but the thinner the air becomes. More than one person has stood at the top and shouted, "Mine is the glory!" only to lose their balance and fall.

The Great House of God

THE WAGES OF SIN
IS DEATH.

Romans 6:23 niv

THE SOUL KILLER

SIN IS A FATAL DISEASE.

Sin has sentenced us to a slow, painful death.

Sin does to a life what shears do to a flower. A cut at the stem separates a flower from the source of life. Initially the flower is attractive, still colorful and strong. But watch that flower over a period of time, and the leaves will wilt and the petals will drop. No matter what you do, the flower will never live again. Surround it with water. Stick the stem in soil. Baptize it with fertilizer. Glue the flower back on the stem. Do what you wish. The flower is dead.

A dead soul has no life.

Cut off from God, the soul withers and dies. The consequence of sin is not a bad day or a bad mood but a dead soul. The sign of a dead soul is clear: poisoned lips and cursing mouths, feet that lead to violence and eyes that don't see God.

Now you know how people can be so vulgar. Their souls are dead. Now you see how some religions can be so oppressive. They have no life. Now you understand how the drug peddler can sleep at night and the dictator can live with his conscience. He has none.

The finished work of sin is to kill the soul.

In the Grip of Grace

SEEMS THAT GOD IS
LOOKING MORE
FOR WAYS TO
GET US HOME
THAN FOR WAYS TO
KEEP US OUT.

GRACE ISN'T LOGICAL

GOD'S JUDGMENT HAS NEVER BEEN a problem for me. In fact, it always seemed right. Lightning bolts on Sodom. Fire on Gomorrah. *Good job, God.* Egyptians swallowed in the Red Sea. *They had it coming.*

Discipline is easy for me to swallow. Logical to assimilate. Manageable and appropriate.

But God's grace? Anything but.

Examples? How much time do you have?

David the psalmist becomes David the voyeur, but by God's grace becomes David the psalmist again.

The thief on the cross: hell-bent and hung out to die one minute, heaven-bound and smiling the next.

Story after story. Prayer after prayer. Surprise after surprise . . .

I challenge you to find one soul who came to God seeking grace and did not find it . . . Find one person who came seeking a second chance and left with a stern lecture.

I dare you. Search.

You won't find it.

When God Whispers Your Name

NOTHING TO
WORLD ABOUT

THE LAST THING WE NEED to worry about is not having enough. Our cup overflows with blessings.

Let me ask a question—a crucial question. If focusing on our diminishing items leads to envy, what would happen if we focused on the unending items? If awareness of what we don't have creates jealousy, is it possible that an awareness of our abundance will lead to contentment?

Let's give it a try and see what happens. Let's dedicate a few paragraphs to a couple of blessings that, according to the Bible, are overflowing in our lives.

"The more we see our sinfulness, the more we see God's *abounding* grace forgiving us" (Romans 5:20 TLB, emphasis mine). To abound is to have a surplus, an abundance, an extravagant portion. Should the fish in the Pacific worry that it will run out of ocean? No. Why? The ocean abounds with water. Need the lark be anxious about finding room in the sky to fly? No. The sky abounds with space.

Should the Christian worry that the cup of mercy will run empty? He may. For he may not be aware of God's abounding grace. Are you? Are you aware that the cup God gives you *overflows* with mercy? Or are you afraid your cup will run dry?

Your warranty will expire? Are you afraid your mistakes are too great for God's grace?

We can't help but wonder if the apostle Paul had the same fear. Before he was Paul the apostle, he was Saul the murderer. Before he encouraged Christians, he murdered Christians. What would it be like to live with such a past?

Did he ever meet children whom he had made orphans?

Did their faces haunt his sleep? Did Paul ever ask, "Can God forgive a man like me?"

The answer to his and our questions is found in a letter he wrote to Timothy: "The grace of our Lord was poured out on me abundantly, along with the faith and love that are in Christ Jesus" (1 Timothy 1:14 NIV).

God is not a miser with his grace. Your cup may be low on cash or clout, but it is overflowing with mercy. You may not have the prime parking place, but you have sufficient pardon. "He will abundantly pardon" (Isaiah 55:7 NKJV). Your cup overflows with grace.

And because it does, your cup overflows with hope. "God will help you overflow with hope in him through the Holy Spirit's power within you" (Romans 15:13 TLB).

Traveling Light

IN GOD'S HANDS
INTENDED EVIL BECOMES
EVENTUAL GOOD.

Stop and Consider
God's Purpose

God is not *sometimes* sovereign. He is not *occasionally* victorious. He does not occupy the throne one day and vacate it the next. "The Lord shall not turn back until He has executed and accomplished the thoughts and intents of His mind" (Jeremiah 30:24 AMP). This season in which you find yourself may puzzle you, but it does not bewilder God. He can and will use it for his purpose.

Every day God tests us through people, pain, or problems. Stop and consider your circumstances. Can you identify the tests of today? Snarling traffic? Threatening weather? Aching joints?

If you see your troubles as nothing more than isolated hassles and hurts, you'll grow bitter and angry. Yet if you see your troubles as tests used by God for his glory and your maturity, then even the smallest incidents take on significance.

You'll Get Through This

"BE STILL, AND KNOW THAT I AM GOD" READS THE SIGN ON GOD'S WAITING ROOM WALL. YOU CAN BE GLAD BECAUSE GOD IS GOOD. YOU CAN BE STILL BECAUSE HE IS ACTIVE. YOU CAN REST BECAUSE HE IS BUSY.

God's Waiting Room

You may be infertile or inactive or in limbo or in between jobs or in search of health, help, a house, or a spouse. Are you in God's waiting room? If so, here is what you need to know: *while you wait, God works.*

"My Father is always at his work," Jesus said (John 5:17 NIV). God never twiddles his thumbs. He never stops. He takes no vacations. He rested on the seventh day of creation but got back to work on the eighth and hasn't stopped since. Just because you are idle, don't assume God is . . .

You'll get through this waiting room season just fine. Pay careful note, and you will detect the most wonderful surprise. The doctor will step out of his office and take the seat next to yours. "Just thought I'd keep you company while you are waiting." Not every physician will do that, but yours will. After all, he is the Great Physician.

You'll Get Through This

PRAISE TO GOD

You are a great God.
Your character is holy.
Your truth is absolute.
Your strength is unending.
Your discipline is fair.
You are a great God.
The mountain of your knowledge has no peak.
The ocean of your love has no shore.
The fabric of your fidelity has no tear.
The rock of your word has no crack.
You are a great God.
Your patience surprises us.
Your beauty stuns us.
Your love stirs us.
You are a great God.
Your provisions are abundant for our needs.
Your light is adequate for our path.
Your grace is sufficient for our sins.
You are a great God.
We even declare with reluctant words, your plan is perfect.
You are never early, never late.
Never tardy, never quick.
You sent your Son in the fullness of time and will return at
*   the consummation of time.*
Your plan is perfect.
Bewildering. Puzzling. Troubling.
But perfect.

From "He Reminded Us of You"
(A Prayer for a Friend)

Two Is Fine
Company

A Friend for the Journey

GOD IS IN YOUR
CORNER

WHEN I WAS SEVEN YEARS OLD, I ran away from home. I'd had enough of my father's rules and decided I could make it on my own, thank you very much. With my clothes in a paper bag, I stormed out the back gate and marched down the alley. Like the prodigal son, I decided I needed no father. Unlike the prodigal son, I didn't go far. I got to the end of the alley and remembered I was hungry, so I went back home.

But though the rebellion was brief, it was rebellion nonetheless. And had you stopped me on that prodigal path between the fences and asked me who my father was, I just might have told you how I felt. I just might have said, "I don't need a father. I'm too big for the rules of my family. It's just me, myself, and my paper bag." I don't remember saying that to anyone, but I remember thinking it. And I also remember rather sheepishly stepping in the back door and taking my seat at the supper table across from the very father I had, only moments before, disowned.

Did he know of my insurrection? I suspect he did. Did he know of my denial? Dads usually do. Was I still his son? Apparently so. (No one else was sitting in my place.) Had you gone to my father after you had spoken to me and asked, "Mr. Lucado, your son says he has no need of a father. Do you still consider him your son?" what would my dad have said?

I don't have to guess at his answer. He called himself my father even when I didn't call myself his son. His commitment to me was greater than my commitment to him.

I didn't hear the rooster crow like Peter did. I didn't feel the fish belch like Jonah did. I didn't get a robe and a ring and sandals like the prodigal did. But I learned from my father on earth what those three learned from their Father in heaven. Our God is no fair-weather Father. He's not into this love-'em-and-leave-'em stuff. I can count on him to be in my corner no matter how I perform. You can too.

The Great House of God

YOU'LL GIVE UP
ON YOURSELF BEFORE
GOD WILL.

BE STILL AND KNOW
THAT I AM GOD

PSALM 46:10

Bury God's Name
in Your Heart

WHEN YOU ARE CONFUSED ABOUT the future, go to your *Jehovah-raah*, your caring shepherd. When you are anxious about provision, talk to *Jehovah-jireh*, the Lord who provides. Are your challenges too great? Seek the help of *Jehovah-shalom*, the Lord is peace. Is your body sick? Are your emotions weak? *Jehovah-rophe*, the Lord who heals you, will see you now. Do you feel like a soldier stranded behind enemy lines? Take refuge in *Jehovah-nissi*, the Lord my banner.

Meditating on the names of God reminds you of the character of God. Take these names and bury them in your heart.

God is:

the shepherd who guides,

the Lord who provides,

the voice who brings peace in the storm,

the physician who heals the sick, and

the banner that guides the soldier.

And most of all, he . . . is.

The Great House of God

IF YOUR GOD IS
MIGHTY ENOUGH TO IGNITE
THE SUN, COULD IT BE
THAT HE IS MIGHTY ENOUGH
TO LIGHT YOUR PATH?

God Is Cheering
for You

GOD IS FOR YOU. NOT "may be," not "has been," not "was," not "would be," but "God is!" He is for you. Today. At this hour. At this minute. As you read this sentence. No need to wait in line or come back tomorrow. He is with you. He could not be closer than he is at this second. His loyalty won't increase if you are better nor lessen if you are worse. He is for you.

God is *for* you. Turn to the sidelines; that's God cheering your run. Look past the finish line; that's God applauding your steps. Listen for him in the bleachers, shouting your name. Too tired to continue? He'll carry you. Too discouraged to fight? He's picking you up. God is *for* you.

God is for *you*. Had he a calendar, your birthday would be circled. If he drove a car, your name would be on his bumper. If there's a tree in heaven, he's carved your name in the bark. We know he has a tattoo, and we know what it says. "I have written your name on my hand," he declares (Isaiah 49:16).

In the Grip of Grace

Do You Hear the Music?

IMAGINE DANCERS WHO HAVE NO MUSIC. Day after day they came to the great hall just off the corner of Main and Broadway. They brought their wives. They brought their husbands. They brought their children and their hopes. They came to dance.

The hall was prepared for a dance. Streamers strung, punch bowls filled. Chairs were placed against the walls. People arrived and sat, knowing they had come to a dance but not knowing how to dance because they had no music. They had balloons; they had cake. They even had a stage on which the musicians could play, but they had no musicians.

One time a lanky fellow claimed to be a musician. He sure looked the part, what with his belly-length beard and fancy violin. All stood the day he stood before them and pulled the violin out of the case and placed it beneath his chin. *Now we will dance*, they thought, but they were wrong. For though he had a violin, his violin had no strings. The pushing and pulling of his bow sounded like the creaking of an unoiled door. Who can dance to a sound like that? So the dancers took their seats again.

Some tried to dance without the music. . . . Over time, however, those dancers grew weary, and everyone resumed the task of sitting and staring and wondering if anything was ever going to happen. And then one day it did.

Not everyone saw him enter. Only a few. Nothing about his appearance would compel your attention. His looks were common, but his music was not. He began to sing a song, soft and sweet, kind and compelling. His song took the chill out of the air and brought a summer-sunset glow to the heart.

And as he sang, people stood—a few at first, then many—and they began to dance. Together. Flowing to a music they had never heard before, they danced.

Some, however, remained seated. What kind of musician is this who never mounts the stage? Who brings no band? Who has no costume? Why, musicians don't just walk in off the street. They have an entourage, a reputation, a persona to project and protect. Why, this fellow scarcely mentioned his name!

"How can we know what you sing is actually music?" they challenged.

His reply was to the point: "Let the man who has ears to hear use them."

But the nondancers refused to hear. So they refused to dance. Many still refuse. The musician comes and sings. Some dance. Some don't. Some find music for life; others live in silence. To those who miss the music, the musician gives the same appeal: "Let the man who has ears to hear use them."

A regular time and place.

An open Bible.

An open heart.

Let God have you, and let God love you—and don't be surprised if your heart begins to hear music you've never heard and your feet learn to dance as never before.

Just Like Jesus

MY ETERNAL SOUL IS UNDER
HEAVENLY COVERAGE,
AND JESUS ISN'T KNOWN
FOR DISMISSING CLIENTS.

What We Really
Want to Know

HERE IS WHAT WE WANT TO KNOW. We want to know how long God's love will endure . . . Not just on Easter Sunday when our shoes are shined and our hair is fixed. We want to know (deep within, don't we really want to know?), how does God feel about me when I'm a jerk? Not when I'm peppy and positive and ready to tackle world hunger. Not then. I know how he feels about me then. Even I like me then.

I want to know how he feels about me when I snap at anything that moves, when my thoughts are gutter-level, when my tongue is sharp enough to slice a rock. How does he feel about me then?

That's what we want to know.

Untethered by time, he sees us all. From the backwoods of Virginia to the business district of London . . . Vagabonds and ragamuffins all, he saw us before we were born.

And he loves what he sees. Flooded by emotion. Overcome by pride, the Starmaker turns to us, one by one, and says, "You are my child. I love you dearly. I'm aware that someday you'll turn from me and walk away. But I want you to know, I've already provided you a way back."

In the Grip of Grace

WHEN JESUS WENT
HOME, HE LEFT THE
FRONT DOOR OPEN.

A Home for Your Heart

Chances are you've given little thought to housing your soul. We create elaborate houses for our bodies, but our souls are relegated to a hillside shanty where the night winds chill us and the rain soaks us. Is it any wonder the world is so full of cold hearts?

It doesn't have to be this way. We don't have to live outside. It's not God's plan for your heart to roam as a Bedouin. God wants you to move in out of the cold and live . . . with him. Under his roof there is space available. At his table a plate is set. In his living room a wingback chair is reserved just for you. And he'd like you to take up residence in his house. Why would he want you to share his home?

Simple, he's your Father.

The Great House of God

IF GOD CARES ENOUGH
ABOUT THE PLANET
SATURN TO GIVE IT RINGS OR
VENUS TO MAKE IT SPARKLE,
IS THERE AN OUTSIDE CHANCE
THAT HE CARES ENOUGH
ABOUT YOU TO MEET YOUR NEEDS?

He Did It for You

Why did God do it? A shack would have sufficed, but he gave us a mansion. Did he have to give the birds a song and the mountains a peak? Was he required to put stripes on the zebra and the hump on the camel? Would we have known the difference had he made the sunsets gray instead of orange? Why wrap creation in such splendor? Why go to such trouble to give such gifts?

Why do you? You do the same. I've seen you searching for a gift. I've seen you stalking the malls and walking the aisles. I'm not talking about the obligatory gifts. I'm not describing the last-minute purchase of drugstore perfume on the way to the birthday party. Forget blue-light specials and discount purchases; I'm talking about that extra-special person and that extra-special gift . . . Why do you do it? You do it so the eyes will pop. You do it so the heart will stop. You do it to hear those words of disbelief, "You did this for *me*?"

That's why you do it. And that is why God did it. Next time a sunrise steals your breath or a meadow of flowers leaves you speechless, remain that way. Say nothing and listen as heaven whispers, "Do you like it? I did it just for you."

The Great House of God

WHAT IS IMPOSSIBLE
WITH MAN IS POSSIBLE
WITH GOD.

WHAT SIZE IS GOD?

NATURE IS GOD'S WORKSHOP. The sky is his résumé. The universe is his calling card. You want to know who God is? See what he has done. You want to know his power? Take a look at his creation. Curious about his strength? Pay a visit to his home address: 1 Billion Starry Sky Avenue . . .

He is untainted by the atmosphere of sin,

unbridled by the time line of history,

unhindered by the weariness of the body.

What controls you doesn't control him. What troubles you doesn't trouble him. What fatigues you doesn't fatigue him. Is an eagle disturbed by traffic? No, he rises above it. Is the whale perturbed by a hurricane? Of course not, he plunges beneath it. Is the lion flustered by the mouse standing directly in his way? No, he steps over it.

How much more is God able to soar above, plunge beneath, and step over the troubles of the earth!

The Great House of God

THE COST OF YOUR SINS IS MORE THAN YOU CAN PAY. THE GIFT OF YOUR GOD IS MORE THAN YOU CAN IMAGINE.

GOD IS YOUR HOME

DON'T THINK YOU ARE SEPARATED from God, he at the top end of a great ladder, you at the other. Dismiss any thought that God is on Venus while you are on Earth. Since God is Spirit (John 4:23), he is next to you: God himself is our roof. God himself is our wall. And God himself is our foundation.

Moses knew this. "Lord," he prayed, "you have been our home since the beginning" (Psalm 90:1). What a powerful thought: God as your home. Your home is the place where you can kick off your shoes and eat pickles and crackers and not worry about what people think when they see you in your bathrobe.

Your home is familiar to you. No one has to tell you how to locate your bedroom; you don't need directions to the kitchen. After a hard day scrambling to find your way around in the world, it's assuring to come home to a place you know. God can be equally familiar to you. With time you can learn where to go for nourishment, where to hide for protection, where to turn for guidance. Just as your earthly house is a place of refuge, so God's house is a place of peace. God's house has never been plundered, his walls have never been breached.

The Great House of God

IN THE CHAPEL
OF WORSHIP WE TAKE
OUR MIND OFF OURSELVES
AND SET IT ON GOD.
THE EMPHASIS IS ON HIM.

Put a Bounce
in Your Step

Some years ago a sociologist accompanied a group of mountain climbers on an expedition. Among other things, he observed a distinct correlation between cloud cover and contentment. When there was no cloud cover and the peak was in view, the climbers were energetic and cooperative. When the gray clouds eclipsed the view of the mountaintop, though, the climbers were sullen and selfish.

The same thing happens to us. As long as our eyes are on God's majesty there is a bounce in our step. But let our eyes focus on the dirt beneath us and we will grumble about every rock and crevice we have to cross. For this reason Paul urged, "Don't shuffle along, eyes to the ground, absorbed with the things right in front of you. Look up, and be alert to the things going on around Christ—that's where the action is. See things from his perspective" (Colossians 3:1–2 MSG).

The Great House of God

FAITH IN THE FUTURE
BEGETS POWER
IN THE PRESENT.

God's Thoughts

We ask for grace, only to find forgiveness already offered. (How did you know I would sin?)

We ask for food, only to find provision already made. (How did you know I would be hungry?)

We ask for guidance, only to find answers in God's ancient story. (How did you know what I would ask?)

God dwells in a different realm . . .

God's thoughts are not our thoughts, nor are they even *like* ours. We aren't even in the same neighborhood. We're thinking, *Preserve the body;* he's thinking, *Save the soul.* We dream of a pay raise. He dreams of raising the dead. We avoid pain and seek peace. God uses pain to bring peace. "I'm going to live before I die," we resolve. "Die, so you can live," he instructs. We love what rusts. He loves what endures. We rejoice at our successes. He rejoices at our confessions. We show our children the Nike star with the million-dollar smile and say, "Be like Mike." God points to the crucified carpenter with bloody lips and a torn side and says, "Be like Christ."

The Great House of God

You Haven't Got a
Prayer Without Prayer

How long has it been since you let God have you? I mean really have you? How long since you gave him a portion of undiluted, uninterrupted time listening for his voice? Apparently Jesus did. He made a deliberate effort to spend time with God.

Spend much time reading about the listening life of Jesus and a distinct pattern emerges. He spent regular time with God, praying and listening. Mark says, "Very early in the morning, while it was still dark, Jesus got up, left the house and went off to a solitary place, where he prayed" (Mark 1:35 NIV). Luke tells us, "Jesus often withdrew to lonely places and prayed" (Luke 5:16 NIV).

Let me ask the obvious. If Jesus, the Son of God, the sinless Savior of humankind, thought it worthwhile to clear his calendar to pray, wouldn't we be wise to do the same?

Not only did he spend regular time with God in prayer, he spent regular time in God's Word. Of course we don't find Jesus pulling a leather-bound New Testament from his satchel and reading it. We do, however, see the stunning example of Jesus, in the throes of the wilderness temptation, using the Word of God to deal with Satan. Three times he is tempted, and each time he repels the attack with the phrase: "It is written in the Scriptures" (Luke 4:4, 8, 12), and then he quotes a verse. Jesus is so familiar with Scripture that he not only knows the verse, he knows how to use it.

And then there's the occasion when Jesus was asked to read in the synagogue. He is handed the book of Isaiah the prophet. He finds the passage, reads it, and declares, "While you heard these words just now, they were coming true!" (Luke 4:21). We are given the picture of a person who knows his way around in Scripture and can recognize its fulfillment. If Jesus thought it wise to grow familiar with the Bible, shouldn't we do the same?

If we are to be just like Jesus—if we are to have ears that hear God's voice—then we have just found two habits worth imitating: the habits of prayer and Bible reading. Consider these verses:

> Base your happiness on your hope in Christ. When trials come endure them patiently; steadfastly maintain *the habit of prayer*. (Romans 12:12 PHILLIPS, emphasis mine)

> The man who looks into the perfect law, the law of liberty, and makes a habit of so doing, is not the man who hears and forgets. He puts that law into practice and he wins true happiness. (James 1:25 PHILLIPS)

If we are to be just like Jesus, we must have a regular time of talking to God and listening to his Word.

Just Like Jesus

ANGELS PROTECTING YOU
ALONG THE WAY

THOUSANDS OF ANGELS AWAITED THE call of Christ on the day of the cross. "Do you think that I cannot appeal to My Father, and He will at once put at My disposal more than twelve legions of angels?" (Matthew 26:53 NASB). One legion equated to six thousand soldiers. Quick math reveals that seventy-two thousand hosts of heaven (enough to fill Los Angeles's Angel Stadium more than one and a half times) stood poised to rescue their Master. The book of Revelation, brimming as it is with glimpses into the soon-to-be world, refers to angels around the heavenly throne, "and the number of them was ten thousand times ten thousand, and thousands of thousands" (Revelation 5:11 NKJV).

If God opened our eyes, what would we see? Moms and dads, you'd see angels escorting your child to school. Travelers, you'd see angels encircling the aircraft. Patients, you'd see angels monitoring the moves of the surgeon. Teenagers, you'd see angels overseeing your sleep. Many, many angels. . . .

God's angels are marked by indescribable strength. Paul says Christ "will come with his mighty angels" (2 Thessalonians 1:7). From the word translated *mighty*, we have the English word *dynamic*. Angels pack dynamic force. It took only one angel to slay the firstborn of Egypt and only one angel to close the mouths of the lions to protect Daniel. David called angels "mighty creatures who carry out his plans, listening for each of his commands" (Psalm 103:20). . . .

Only one sight enthralls angels—God's face. They know that he is Lord of all. And as a result, they worship him. Whether in the temple with Isaiah or the pasture with the Bethlehem shepherds, angels worship. "When he presented his honored Son to the world, God said, 'Let all the angels of God worship Him'" (Hebrews 1:6 NKJV). They did and they do.

Remember the earlier reference to the ten thousand times ten thousand angels encircling the throne of heaven? Guess what they are doing? The Bible says, "All the angels stood around the throne . . . saying: 'Amen! Blessing and glory and wisdom, thanksgiving and honor and power and might, be to our God forever and ever. Amen'" (Revelation 7:11–12 NKJV).

Doesn't that proclaim volumes about God's beauty? Angels could gaze at the Grand Tetons and Grand Canyon, Picasso paintings and the Sistine Chapel, but they choose, instead, to fix their eyes on the glory of God. They can't see enough of him, and they can't be silent about what they see.

At the very moment you read these words, God's sinless servants offer unceasing worship to their Maker. He is, remember, their creator. At one time no angels existed. And then, by God's decree, they did. "He made the things we can see and the things we can't see—kings, kingdoms, rulers, and authorities. Everything has been created through him and for him" (Colossians 1:16). Angels fill God's invisible creation.

They worship him, and—here is a drink for thirsty hearts— they protect us. "All the angels are spirits who serve God and are sent to *help those who will receive salvation*" (Hebrews 1:14, emphasis mine).

Come Thirsty

God's Grace Is
Sufficient

Plunge a sponge into Lake Erie. Did you absorb every drop? Take a deep breath. Did you suck the oxygen out of the atmosphere? Pluck a pine needle from a tree in Yosemite. Did you deplete the forest of foliage? Watch an ocean wave crash against the beach. Will there never be another one?

Of course there will. No sooner will one wave crash into the sand than another appears. Then another, then another. This is a picture of God's sufficient grace. *Grace* is simply another word for his tumbling, rumbling reservoir of strength and protection. It comes at us not occasionally or miserly but constantly and aggressively, wave upon wave. We've barely regained our balance from one breaker, and then, *bam*, here comes another.

"Grace upon grace" (John 1:16 NASB). We dare to hang our hat and stake our hope on the gladdest news of all: if God permits the challenge, he will provide the grace to meet it.

We never exhaust his supply. "Stop asking so much! My grace reservoir is running dry." Heaven knows no such words . . .

Take all your anxieties to Calvary, Paul urged. Stand in the shadow of God's crucified Son. Now pose your questions. *Is Jesus on my side?* Look at the wound in his. *Will he stay with me?* Having given the supreme and costliest gift, "how can he fail to lavish upon us all he has to give?" (Romans 8:32 NEB).

Let God's grace dethrone your fears. Anxiety still comes, for certain. The globe still heats up; wars still flare up; the economy acts up. Disease, calamity, and trouble populate your world. But they don't control it! Grace does.

Grace

GOD HAS ENOUGH GRACE
TO SOLVE EVERY
DILEMMA YOU FACE, WIPE
EVERY TEAR THAT YOU CRY,
AND ANSWER EVERY
QUESTION YOU ASK.

God's Love for You

Human love is convenient. It suits the needs of the person at the time and works into his schedule.

God's love is eternal. You are always on God's itinerary. Come and go as you wish, but he's always there.

Human love is limited. It can love only as much as it wants to give.

God's love is unlimited. He has ample amounts of love and even uses words like *abundant* when talking about pouring out his love on people.

Human love is emotional. Feelings dominate a human's love landscape. We feel as though we're in love, or we don't feel as though we're in love. Hormones, sleeplessness, worry, past hurts, Mexican food—all complicate these emotions.

God's love is committed. While God has feelings for us, his feelings don't dictate his love. His love is based on a decision to love us. Your actions don't increase or decrease his commitment. His love is a deeper and more secure love than the fluctuating Ferris wheel of feeling.

Human love is selfish. It must suit our needs and be there for us. To love, we must be loved.

God's love is unselfish. In fact, if you never love God, he will still love you. Your love has no bearing on the amount of love he lavishes on you.

One thing human love has going for it is that you can see it—in the twinkling of your father's eye, in the smile of a spouse, in the joy in your children's voices.

God's love is just as real but not as tangible. We will see it, in time and for eternity, as we gaze at the face of God and his Son, Jesus Christ, while we stand in his presence in heaven.

Max on Life

YOU ARE LOVED BY YOUR MAKER NOT BECAUSE YOU TRY TO PLEASE HIM AND SUCCEED, OR FAIL TO PLEASE HIM AND APOLOGIZE, BUT BECAUSE HE WANTS TO BE YOUR FATHER.

Teach Us to Pray

Our Father

Thank you for adopting me into your family.

who is

Thank you, my Lord,

for being a God of the present tense:

my Jehovah-jireh (the God who provides),

my Jehovah-raah (the caring Shepherd),

my Jehovah-shalom (the Lord is peace),

my Jehovah-rophe (the God who heals),

and my Jehovah-nissi (Lord, my banner).

in heaven,

Your workshop of creation reminds me: If you can make the skies, you can make sense out of my struggles.

Hallowed be thy name.

Be holy in my heart.

You are a "cut above" all else.

Enable me to set my sights on you.

Thy kingdom come,

Come kingdom!

Be present, Lord Jesus!

Have free reign in every corner of my life.

Thy will be done,

Reveal your heart to me, dear Father.

Show me my role in your passion.

On earth as it is in heaven.

Thank you that you silence heaven to hear my prayer.

Give us this day our daily bread.

I accept your portion for my life today.

I surrender my concerns regarding my well-being.

Forgive us our debts,

I thank you for the roof of grace over my head,

bound together with the timbers and nails of Calvary.

There is nothing I can do to earn or add to your mercy.

I confess my sins to you.

As we also have forgiven our debtors;

Treat me, Father, as I treat others.

Lead us not into temptation,

Let my small hand be engulfed in yours.

Hold me lest I fall.

Our Father . . . give us . . . forgive us . . . lead us

Let your kindness be on all your church.

I pray especially for ministers near

and missionaries far away.

Thine—not mine—is the kingdom,

I lay my plans at your feet.

Thine—not mine—is the power,

I come to you for strength.

Thine—not mine—is the glory,

I give you all the credit.

Forever. Amen.

The Great House of God

CHARTING YOUR COURSE

First Steps

A Prayer for My Life

PERSONAL · PROFESSIONAL
SPIRITUAL GOALS

three-month goals _____
_____
_____
_____
_____
_____

six-month goals _____
_____
_____
_____
_____
_____

one-year goals _____
_____
_____
_____
_____
_____

two-year goals _____

_____

_____

_____

_____

four-year goals _____

_____

_____

_____

_____

lifetime goals _____

_____

_____

_____

_____

STEPS I HAVE TAKEN TO
REACH MY GOALS:

three-month goals _____

_____

_____

_____

_____

_____

six-month goals _____

_____

_____

_____

_____

_____

one-year goals _____

_____

_____

_____

_____

_____

two-year goals _____

_____

_____

_____

_____

_____

four-year goals _____

_____

_____

_____

_____

_____

lifetime goals _____

_____

_____

_____

_____

_____

Words to Remember:

Favorite Scripture, Quotes, Poems, Sayings

NOTES